where's katie?
elaine feeney

salmonpoetry

Published in 2010 by
Salmon Poetry
Cliffs of Moher, County Clare, Ireland
Website: www.salmonpoetry.com
Email: info@salmonpoetry.com

ISBN 978-1-907056-43-7

Cover design: *Ray Glasheen*
Cover photograph: *Constance Markievicz (1868–1927)*
Typesetting: *Siobhán Hutson*
Printed in England by imprint*digital*.net

Salmon Poetry receives financial assistance from the Arts Council

God Bless Mammy, Daddy, Shane, Elaine, Kenneth, Mark, Andrea, Sandy, the two Nana's, Da and Chief, and Bless This House and Keep It Safe,

Amen.

Acknowledgements

Thanks to the editors of the following publications in which some of these poems were previously published:

The SHOp, Against The Wall, EYEWEAR, Súil Siar, Nth Position, Xposed and *OneSheet*.

The poem, "Urban Myths and the Galway Girl" won the 2008 Cúirt Festival Poetry Grand Slam.

Special thanks to Jessie and Siobhán at Salmon Poetry.

Huge love and thanks to Dave Lordan, Amanda Coakley, Ray Glasheen, Noelle and Phil Moran and Aaron Copeland.

I really appreciate all the wonderful support I have received from my family and friends, and I am especially grateful to all the people involved in poetry and literature in Galway and beyond who have encouraged me to keep going.

And finally to all who have come and listened to many a performance in the small hours of the morning in some den or roadside or smoking area or backroom or empty bar or field or castle from Limerick to Lipica and beyond, Thank You.

Contents

The Red Tractor

You lifted his red tractor to feed the recycling bin
to morph it into a Lidl bag or a coke bottle or a condom.
The engine was missing
and the dog had mushed the horn.
The hitch was being used
as a fork in a fat hand
to hold sausages.

Preserve it! I pleaded,
for I will ride upon it
when I'm buckled and stoned—
eating my teeth and packing mud in my cracks,
and my two boys are in the real world
as cowboys kissing Indians.

Rape

Near me a child is raped in a bog.

I was so ashamed I had almost let us die.

The West sleeps while they reconstruct her.

Raped at six goes so beyond

Goes beyond my think

To the bloodied bog

To media silence

To our silence

To baby tears

Baby fears

Unthink.

Laying Hens

'We are laying hens – be done with it,'
she said, bloody cheek of her.

But then Teresa spoke
over cold cheap coffee,
of female mutilations,
of tribal kings taking
virgins to cure a virus.
So while the West's awake,
ten year olds die with choking children
stuck in immature canals.

Women of the World Unite!
Fight the quiet.

Our Very Own Republic

I

A small woman told me about the mystery train.
Their annual holiday—
twelve apostles up a council avenue
to a pissed-on bus stop,
telling those who could read
that *Johnny loved Rose.*

Past the net curtains
Past the flat builders
Past the church
Past the stained glass flickers throwing light
Past the grey lit up pavement
Past the chippers
Past the paper shop
Past the deaf cobblers

(Waving in with gauche
sign language
at the cobbler
who only heard the silence,
of men throwing boots and shoes
and whatever came to hand)

They envied his mute deafness.
What peace in his silence,
for he could always close his eyes,
but who can close their ears?

To a train stop.
To a rural country stop.

II

Stop talking
Stop going to school
Stop laughing
Stop sleeping in your bed
Stop childhood

(head shoulders knees and toes
head shoulders knees and toes
eyes and ears no mouth and a nose
head shoulders knees and toes)

The Opus Dei men with their shiny shoes—
with their pretty girl children skipping
to Dev! Dev! Dev!
Vote, Vote, Vote for De Valera!

III

The mystery train chugged along the track.

Older ones shoved dummies in the mouths
of snotty ones.
A mother licked her hand
and swept a boy's hair to the side,
strand by strand.

And a mother wore high heels and
fake cashmere.

And another mother in her mass outfit!
Her mass outfit.

To turn the others green with envy!

Vote, vote, vote for De Valera!

IV

We're hard-working men,
ordinary men.
Look where we got
and the boulders knocked from our shoulders—
knocked from shoulders!

Some could have had any man they wanted;
waltzing men,
men with cars and cologne.

The Redemptoristman told them to shut their mouth
        and do their duty.
The coalman winked at them from a toothless grin,
rumour he put cigarettes out on his kids.
The doctorman shrugged his sly shoulders and coughed.
A fatherman asked what the fuck was going on?
The tinkerman sighed and said he's up to his eyes.
The barman told them to post a half crown on a Friday.
And was the most sympathetic,
seeing as he wasn't a drinkingman a'tall.

The Godman never replied—
not once.

The mystery train chugged the guts from the women,
and them wiping the snot clear,
the tears dry,
the pain away,
to the rocks and the stones on
the empire track all the way to Kerry.
For the mystery to be revealed.

Tis your times that are in it
and ye on a mystery train.
Get out, get out!
I'll take them
straight to the home.

Oh by Jesus missus I'll take them if
there's another mouth to feed,
plenty of poor childless feckers
would like one of your
beauties, dragged like half-priced
crippled Christmas toys,
in this Our Very Own Republic.

Upstanding Citizens Murdered by Son in County Tipperary

No one could save me from those kids at school
They would bully, haunt me, taunt me,
You're such a pretty boy.

(Josh Rouse)

I can hear
I can see

This is no country for anyman—
Yeats you fucking pansy!
The young are dying in one another's arms.
Yeats, you fucking pansy!
The young are dying in one another's arms.

His body slumped on hers,
like the broken see-saw
of my childhood,
his body slumped on hers.

Tonight
I won't turn
this on myself.

Point-to-Point

The devil should have bit this
county away,
but I'm fastened between his nibble and
The Rock of Cashel.

Races over, overturned bets betted.
White marquee marks land, like
a snap of a fat ewe taken from heaven.

Acres to a dwelling.

Man Boys stuffed in Wellingtons,
covered in spent animal shite.
Men with remote friendless beards,
slight suspicious jockeys
with belaboured faces.
Sturdy turnip women sip tea from polystyrene cups.
Bullets blow blooded brains out of
Tipperary half-breds.

Huge thicks of men
clasp hands on this foreign Galway girl
who drinks whiskey on the rocks.
The turnip women drop scalding
tea on heated brains of babes
who cling to their paisley skirts.

Screeching!

Whiskey with ice only;
shame on her,
bad things will happen.

Castles

Coloured murky shell holes slurp.
In the hotel lobby
you spotted the girls from earlier,
those from the shallow turquoise pool
where splashes were framed by rubber rings.
She had dark braids and burning flesh,
an-eight-year-old-hard-sider.

You approached her to
tell her you were four—
but she told you to
fuck your four little years
back across the pavilion,
you were wrecking her buzzing braids and
sucking the last drop of light from her moon.

You marched back to me,
beautifully olive,
small fists clenched,
salted tears being swallowed hard
to quench your heart.
You said your eyes must have messed up.
She was the wrong girl.

Thunderous hooves grinded over my
canvas that night.
I saw girls at wooden horses and rubber mats
with their tongues out.

I have feverish dreams of their faces,
mottled and pasty marching away.
Of dead cockroaches put in my denim pocket.
Of days wandering

searching for places to hide my hands,
the only visible skin,
save half a face.

Teachers orated my poems
to desk slumped moans of menstruating girls,
they had black bras under white shirts,
cool long skirts,
Doc Martens with a thousand holes.

And me with a sharp face
and a cloudy awkward pain.
But now come and I'll fuck you
away from any temple
and little hard-north-south-insiders
can show me small fists,
even at eight.

Because it's late
and there is only you and I,
and a stone swirled sky of all I ever
dreamed for you.

Patience
brown eyes
freedom

enough sense to filter trust
but enough elated emotion to feel most of it.
All the wonderful ways that rays
of light flash through this
playdough globe.
Where everyone sees you under a sticky lacquer,
where girls will toss your hair
and speak of green nature,
and how when they feel it,
it's like they've never felt it before;

rain on their face,
warm sour milk
and a pizza dribbled with pesto.

Then Jack you'll realise that the best ones
are the ones who let you
foam and roam
and play,
and be in a single sense.
Coin-like with a rustic value.

When you stand at life's canvas of bright orange,
when heavy disposable everythings
fill up the filtered sound,
then braided selfish siders will
rise through their stupidity.

You were only four.
You only wanted to tell it.
You only wanted to blow ash to sticky icing.

But I dream forever,
for nothing I can do can ever crease the lump
that builds and grows,
like the castles we make.

Cool water will come and wash it
all away to an eternity of grit.

But there are flashes saving
the darkness and halting the ages.

Love

If Love were served as a mojito with ice,
I would shove its leaves
to the recess of my throat
and beg for mercy.

If Love hid in the patterns of this wallpaper,
we could sausage ourselves between
paisley shapes and flock gently together.

If Love were hidden between tree rings in this cabinet,
I would lock myself into its whore-scented drawers
and moisten from the touch of dehydrated forests.

But I share this cave with
bastard bats,
I will hang myself upsidedown
and rejoice when the battle guns outside
stop hurling death.

If I wait,
I will die here.

Unloved and upside down.

Mark

You should be my last regret
so I'll give you love
and candy cigarettes.

On a grainy wet
Wednesday of the
Leaving Cert
you were almost convinced the chipped pencil
from Covent Garden, with faded flowers,
would do you for the 'test'—
shir it could draw a line!

And maybe a box.

In two dimensions
(those of love and hate)

And shir the protractor
might have had a chipped corner—

but shir now well life's
not a straight line
a long road with no turns
like a box of chocolates
only we never had chocolates
maybe a leather satchel
at Christmas
or an orange
like the Africans
like the monkeys
in the trees
sucking the life

Counting out inches.

But your friend, he
cut you a lump from his 2H
to save you the embarrassment of using a
pencil from Covent Garden
with lead for a Junior Infant.

And your designs were enough to scare the smile
of the Mona Lisa and hope out of
Da Vinci himself!

You will be my last regret so
I give you love and candy cigarettes.

Spoils of War

Ripped stockings were hung from a palm-top
in the hopeless hope that the killings would stop.

Male children were nestled in Kurd scarves snug,
blurred visions of sugar plums flashed as we dug.

And Mamma teared her kerchief as I removed my bat,
and so turned off my brain for a long winter's nap—

When out on the dirt track there arose such a clatter,
we sprang to mass graves to see what was the matter.

They frothed and fired, I knew like a flash,
I dug open some wounds from their infamous clash.

(Genitals in the mouths of boys holding hands with
fathers bound hard from their wrists to these lands)

Heads with top teeth
Heads with no teeth

The moon, on the beast of new fallen sand snow,
gave the luster of midday to the bones below.

When, what to my wondering eyes should appear;

Bazrani bread filled their pockets from fear
to leave bread trails for mothers
to leave bread trails for lovers

for bread trails
rotted entrails.

More rapid than eagles his coursers they came,
and whistled and shouted and shot them by name.

From the top of their village to the end home wall,
murdered them murdered them murdered them all.

A Crush

The women tell me
that I should keep it all
going.
I should not wear *the shame* anymore.

Strange Fruit

After Sojourner Truth

Orange is my favourite colour,
but the Dutch stole it,
like the Union Jack the flowers dyed
into my mantle-place.

They stole your orange too,
in a whipping pain,
segregation and dull sunshine,
dipped in east-coast-rain.

They stole your siblings,
locked them in a sleigh,
like trunks now deep in sea water,
chained to wrangled seaweed—
plonked Liberty on it and
weakened the hold.

Seaweed stalks now break like Peter's body.

Chains of inhumanity
lay unsettled as damaged
souls huddle in scrums,
grabbing bony fingers broken from labour
and standing on ricketed legs
stapled to tree trunks,
where they hang your progeny
and mute your voice.
Trees now over ducking stools,
silence once gurgled over the speaking woman.

The fires burned her
now trees hang her alibi
and sleighs ride off
through dusky sun with her fruit.

They hang Truth on trees

The *strange fruit*;
and strange ways they thought
they could hide the truth.

Juxtaposition

The juxtaposition of the world

On a bright billboard
On the side of the ditch
On the road at Ballybrit
On the way to the Galway Races

Just a position we have taken

Naked toddlers
choking on Swarovski crystals

We have thrown them away
to sugar-coat the top
of our butter mountains.

Eyre Square Trees

As I stretch, crushed rock
falls through my brittle fingers.
I breathe deep through flat green
palates, then violently shake.

My lungs fall in July now,
a globe warms
and dances for night.
This Mardi Gras will take my lungs,
the breath of this city.

Urban Myths and the Galway Girl

She tells us as we jump
about like idiots—
it was so cold this morning she
thought the Holocaust was upon her—
and she'd just failed her driving test
again
because she couldn't follow around a rear window,
shir that's a ridiculous thing to do
she'd be in the sea,
because he'd brought her around
Ballyloughane
and that's no place to be!
She loves the way the globe is warming
loveeeeen
the heat is lovely.
She had a crush on the bus driver who took
the Castlelawn-Eyre-Square-Salthill
Skeff-for-a-quick-one-route
but ended up with the TV man who came to
fix her father's Ferguson once a year.
He told her that this Christmas
she'd need to tart herself up—

The Fat Bastard—

But they've nice bling in River Island
so she'll tog out there
loveeeeen
even if he is a fat bastard—
shir ya have to keep them happy.
But lately she muses,
she's gone off her husband.
He walks around the house in tracksuit pants
loveeeeeeen
with his sweaty limp bollix hanging sideways,
'tis enough to turn a nun off'
but he's great for the painting
and cleaning out the ashes all the same.

She tells me the youngest with Autism is
growing out of it.
And again she tells me about the foreign national
who left the buggy at the bus stop
only this time she's set it in Salthill and not Mervue.

She's the queen of Urban Myths.

She wishes she had a car and could get this five grand
for the taxi
that the *coloured* lads are getting.
Quote
unquote
she's saying *coloured* because she knows
I'm a bit funny about racism.

She tells us about Jimmy her boss.
It's complicated she says;
you have to let him think he's one up on ya
and then have one up on him
and you'll be one up –
I think.
Then catch him out.

She's four stone loveeeen
she has an overactive thyroid
an underactive husband
a touch of type two diabetes
an overanxious daughter
the odd outbreak of psoriasis
a query of meningo-cockal-cock-something
and definite insanity.

Everywhere in Galway waters down her vodka.
She'll tell Pauline that Christine is a wench
she'll tell Christine that Pauline is loose.
She tells me about all the pills the husband is taking
for the cough and the limp dick and all

nothing is working
loveeeeen.
Now she couldn't care if he went in his sleep.

She's fond of the new pope but not the look of him
loveeeeen
Fond of roundabouts
loveeeeen
The twenty per cent off at Tescos
loveeeeen
She thinks Billy on Eastenders did very well for himself
loveeeeen
But they should really drown that Gail from Corrie
loveeeeen
She's interested in organic veg the oddtime
loveeeeen
Read they were great for constipation
loveeeeen
Because she has piles like a bunch of grapes
and a box so itchy she could feck it out a window.

And finally she gives me a Six Star Plan
for the Perfect Me;
My nails would look great with false tips
My eyes with false lashes
My skin with fake bake
My teeth with fake bleach
My abdomen with fake liptrim
My vagina with a sneaky tuck.

But my boobs are grand,
grand altogether,
loveeeeen!

Who is Writing?

For Piet and Goran

—Nature will never write here
to damage the perfect
when all around has written and damaged,
you do not write for nature
this is where its beauty lies—

A woman writes
A stubborn pretty child writes
A bullied infant writes
An angry father speaks
A history teacher tells of the Gaelic Revival

My ex-husband writes two conclusive lists
My good points
My bad points

They are written
He is writing
The kitchen clock writes

Beautiful women write

Sweat writes
Breasts write

The traveller woman believes in angels—
writes her name for the first time

The dead hunger strikers smile at me—
they don't want anything written down

A man on fire writes

God writes

I am the author
I am the cat sponge

—*Nature will never write here*
to damage the perfect
when all around has written and damaged,
you do not write for nature
this is where its beauty lies—

Pause

Pause.

Standing glaring at characters to the front of your stage.
Velvet tresses from your hair roll to your frock.

Pause.

A pianist fingers tunes to fit your mood,
no note low enough.

I expect any moment that you shall lift your skirt
and scream,
drawing all your cats to the castle

and then you'll smile.

Pause.

And indisciplined flashes will roll under your eyes
as they take revenge on the Slovenian men you've kissed.

Exeunt Stage.

Friday the Thirteenth

For Ray

There are certain things I should avoid on this date.

Hospitals for example.

I wonder how many babies die here?
Unidentifiable body parts,
tiny limbs flushed through the Newcastle waterways,
as empty tears fall from mothers on the
cracked
whitebidetbowl.

I hold onto the sink—
my world is going black again.
Ray comes to me on a white horse,
he's sitting with a cup of sugary tea
outside the chapel,
when I can see again.

Maternity pads on the floor,

this is the undeveloped world,
a cage I cannot escape.
They'll listen for the heartbeat,
given the fall and all,

the woman in number three screams
at her husband to leave.

They want to move me to Beaumont,
the midwives are nervous,
they're nurses, not Gods,
and with a skeleton staff.

Over the phone I reassure my mum,
I'm moistening my hands well,
oh yeah and my neck,
no mum, no one wants a turkey neck.
She's quiet.
She'll be in later,
do I need anything?
More moisturiser maybe?

The baby punches my belly,
the boys arrive with flowers
and a wheelchair.
They have been catching fish
and putting the final touches on
what it means to be a dad
and a stepdad.

Hope.
It means hope.

Jack was wondering were some
fish in the canal half-brothers.

I drift away to a consultant
reading my brain scans
in Roly's, gorging on whale and fish eggs.
I wonder if I were his daughter
would the eggs stick in his throat.

Whitebidetbowls.
Maternity pads on the floor.
A cage.
Ray drinking sugary tea.
Jack's reflection in the canal.
Mum and Dad will visit.

Undeveloped.
A cage.

I can't ask me da

'I can't ask me da for nothing!

NotfornothinNotforpyjamasorCalpoloraMrFreeze

or fishes and calculators
Playstation games

I can't ask me da for nothin
not for nothin
not for a Capri-Sun
or socks

or where babies come from
or runners
an electric guitar
or how to spell Mother
or mammy
or her new home with Kevin—
In the sky
with Kevin—
In the sky
with Kevin—
Mammy's in the sky with Kevin
oh mammy
From the ska
the ska sent her to Kevin—
that's what me da says

me da doesn't like Kevin
so now I can't ask him for nothin
not nothin
I can't ask me da for nothing.
Not nothin'.

Women

*At least my women were something to write about and that
was just about the extent of it*
    —Charles Bukowski

The tall fella with the African Lynx
and yellowing fingers,
keeps shouting,
'faggots are fruits.'

And his father agrees.

But they excuse this with an offering—
women.
Although they've met a fair share of whores and tarts—
they don't discriminate against women—
they'd catch a falling star
or throw their coat over a puddle,

for their woman.

Marietta

Oh Marietta!
Amongst the hard snakes
and cloudy sky schnapps,
between clotted marble tiles
and fading green juiced limes.

Oh Marietta!
Amongst miniature trains
and brains deflated,
squeezing oiled skin
under this freckled sky.

Floor Polishing

Wide strokes on the floors you polished
so late at night, for less than the price of a bottle
of wine,
yet your pride takes hold of everything
as an octopus takes hold of reflecting light
in the coming dawn.

Polish rises—

Waiting for a cheque.
Waiting for a cheque.

Reflections in January

This is the most depressing day of the year.

Official.

And the monkey on my back is a piece of chipped glass
        stuck in my dishwasher
and a Spiderman web is stuck to my washing machine.

I write a letter to my Nigerian friend
I do not ask after unmarked graves
I do not ask after her missing husband
I do not ask her children's names

I enclose a picture of us all
in Santa's grotto.

Fresh Cut Flowers

Just a little green
ice and some birthday cards.

There'll be no more
fresh cut flowers in the
kitchen now her mum is dead.

Dead flowers.

War March

I powder my face
I bleach my hair
I make myself other
I'm not without fault
I'm not into hurtling rocks
I march in line with others

Those who isolate speech bubbles,
stone throwers,
unshaven men in ribbed khaki hoodies,
girls in the Hijab,
pimply ones with grungy gunk,
women in gypsy skirts tell me they're learning Arabic.

I chat, but they're still suspicious.
I'd never been to Dachau
or Palestine.
Homes in Palestine,
As large rusty keys are stolen off old men.
Earlier on our history timeline
I show the first years panic-fuelled
diamonds swallowed whole in unleavened bread in the
        Warsaw ghetto.
I don't show them a Nazi officer raping an escapee
as hoards of skinny women
try to keep their babies quiet,
by filling their tiny mouths with sharp stars.

It's a copycat.
As usual. To keep
the rats running the wheel.

The rain has repelled the crowd
on O'Connell Street.
We pass the post office,

busy in Penney's.
Children skip brightly through coloured anoraks,
trip to the pavement.
Watch the Landmines.
Oh no wrong country. Skip away.

In the dark distant of flakes and berries,
of lucky green herbs,
can we still feel our

isolation
desolation
interrogation

now it foams our fattening skin
and blood glistens from the eyes of other children.

American army planes glide through
Shannon with six-pack
flat-top
boys, awakened from their wet dream
on an island far from Idaho and East Virginia.
Buying silly sheep t-shirts
and Guinness key-rings.
Is this it?
Is this the sum of our freedom?

If my hell has words
it's saying my ears are no longer Switzerland,
my country is no longer on the uplands,
this island is no longer a timid young brother.

Go march, for
softheaded children
die everywhere.
In weathers of erosion
In melting heat
Behind full flock curtains

Beneath thin steel wire
In ghetto-wall-holes
Between tall concrete graffiti slabs
Under cold dark moons
In tiger clubs
In stone huts
On desert strips
In pink brothels
Under truck bonnets.

They groan for their mothers,
their baby brothers are crawling on their hands and their knees.

We scream for a powerful
sea to calm this boiling blood

For fairy tales
For books with pictures
For pastel blocks and bright shapes
For streets again with full fruit trees
For pyjamas without stripes
For apple berries
For the tooth fairy
For a few ships of salvation.

Peace.

A simple thing.

Cork

Saturday night, near marching season,
knee trembling experiences.
A full peep show on Panna.

(Outside Waterstones)

Where half a day earlier
pretty children ate vanilla
ice cream and froze dreams
of ducks they had fed
at the Mardyke.

(With stale glass encased bread)

Suburbanised rockers spat abuse and
rolled their skinny tight asses
to the city for a tear.

Foolish fucks.

I stroll down piss-riddled streets
through a gauntlet of comments

to another country

where already I'm dead and unburied.

Where I'm nothing but teeth and charred rind in a clearing.

Or I'm nailed to the wall

in an outhouse

arms akimbo

legs spread

unidentifiable

to all but the chief of the rapist police.

My accent didn't suit your cochlea boy
like your flea cock for the airscrew bitches
you chew.

Kicks on an empty stomach with
cheap pimp market shoes.
You could pimp me to the
necrophilist because I'd drown in congealed
blood before I'd ever let you have me.

I'm left on the path
up Oliver Plunkett Street.
I taught your kids,
they asked after my scars.

On Gilmartin Road

they chuck children out
with the bath water in front
of high-speed Japanese imports.

This is the road where horses flag
down on old flock armchairs.

Where Maggie's sitting room is adorned with a bronze
touch lantern, and a three-piece suite sits on
the mossy lawn of number sixty-six.

Where children follow children's children
out to the middle of muddle lane.

They own it, for they live in terrace
of houses with one attic,
the unshod horse rules.

So it was in the nineteen hundreds,
and it's a highway code kept

out of posterity
and fear.

Irish Country Girl Visits Tate Modern

I am giggly from Frascati before noon.

Dull Thames deadness
mutes orange butterflies
lapping in my belly
feeding on chorizo chew.

Shoving a sugar coated thumb in and
out of a tired teething mouth
of pain and separation, but he's
asleep in another country.

Lilac oil on a soaked canvas,
hard nipples in taut grey shapes,
soft steps in this poorhouse gallery
brainwashed clean with eroding peoples.

Genitalia of a plastic lobster
engage the receiver,
numb as the Tupperware
your mother saved for.

I'm a watching woman watching you
pulling at the drawers from a dig—
a cabinet of stolen mahogany air
china dolls, dinky cars, clay pipes and fag boxes.

Drowned to the bottom of her waters,
so many stories,
dredged without asking
gaping at lavandered souls,

My salted irritated torso.
I'm a pervert on her banks at midnight
as young unshaven faces
eyes bright as duffel buttons dance away.

You like the technical aspects of print,
attempting to understand process.
Joan Miro is a blast from ninety-six,
but the cabinet holds our attention.

Where's Katie?

for Mum

Some woman's yellow hair has maddened every mother's son

WB Yeats

I have, have I?
We've revved and motored past a second coming,
all the talk of war and comings
speaks of threes and thirds now.

With six thousand percent peroxide
blistering my scalp
not Matthew, Mark, Luke or John
would have me now.

Since I have withered.

I am damaged.
I am interrupted.
I am dying.

It's all over.
Ye feckless stupid fools that did
me, that I watched,
helpless on a stone on the prom,
I should've jumped into it years ago,
the black unknown,
where even my clothes would have come undone.

For greed, for greed, for greed.

I'm so sorry boys
they say the Stone Breakers
is busy with wailing

spirits, screaming in agony.
I'd visit, but toothless and bleached—
I'm too ashamed.

I am waist deep,
is there an end to this futile preening?

Like a swan blacked out in an oil slick
I'll poison myself with my own tongue.

This awful thirst,
the more I drink.

This awful thirst,
the more I drink.

I will drink this well dry;
then scale the cathedral spire
fire off tarry hawkers
at holy sisters and archbishops

but there are no churches left for climbing,

only cakes to stick these captured spires through.

So I spread my arms and stand aloft on rain tins
and jig, screeching.

No one understands.

I walk the shut down railway lines
and pile up sleepers.
Sniff lines of crystal up
my septum sides.
Indignant runts splashed from my loins
lie incapable of understanding.
Universally decayed as infants,
babies born

from pathetic poisons are
positioned in comforts away from
root cries of needs.

Haunting hunger!

Oh hunger!
Oh hunger!

My yellowed hands
are cupping nothing.

Ask for this land again,
go on, dare ye, ye cowardly fucks,
for a heaving great giant to lie on me
and let me go,
breed something magical,
and let me come.

He could hook each of these limestones
from the insufferable stonewalls,
he could hurl each one from a tight rod line
into the water.

Each morning the giant could take them,
fished and hooked from the four cornered bed
we lie on, with wrapped limbs and soaking skin,
he could chip at the piece of broken mirror,
that reflects an empty mouth of
broken canines,
and punch the lot endlessly out!
One coarse stone after another,
into the black Atlantic,
the mirror edges chipped away to nothing.
Beat away our stone dead babies,
the useless divided corners that sink the middle
of our four-pieced cause.

Our way now is a cause far down from giants,
to the little people.

I see little people with no eyes.
I see little people with no eyes.

But only mirrors
miming the maddening
curse of this froth,
this fierce froth.

Interrupt me

I am dying

Take me

Bathe me

Take me

Lubricate my line

My life

Unleash me

Unchain me

Unleash the

hidden side

of my

end.

Break Up/ Break Down

The weight of the world is love
Allen Ginsberg

Monday I race,
legs like dead weights under my over-sized body,
I flop to the pavement.

Tuesday I scream but my mouth's dry,
and a burning throat
lumps and lodges.

Wednesday I bite hard on the scentless air
and chip away the
enamel.

Thursday I leap free off the edge of Dun Aengus,
wake with a dead jerk,
kick him out.

Friday I strip naked,
scrawl on the lino,
scavenge the outhouse for my old feather pillow.

Saturday I define and select
from my domestic arsenal
and sit behind the door.

Waiting.
Watching.
Ready.

Sunday I lie stuffing sweet and sour
Chinese chicken balls in my eye sockets.

The contest is open.

Finding Katie Inside the Lap Dancing Pub

I stumbled on the den,
peeled on my row face,
smashed sweat clear
from beneath my weeping eyelids.

A couple of couples
sat on the edge of their stools
and sipped stale apples.

Here she was,
moving like the boy in the bubble.

They felt her breasts through thick sterile black gloves.

Men's eyes ran salty sweat between her bone thighs
and held moisture behind her Estonian pupils
with fumbling childlike paws.

I'd smash their heads in if she was my sister,
even if she said she loved it—
If she was my sister
I'd break their beaks for them,
they could suck it through a straw.

If she were my mother—
I'd blow my own brains out.

So I weaved and waved
to the edge of reason,
where martyrs tipped their hats.

They barred me.
I lost my tenner,
they locked their door
hid inside from me.

I caught a bouncer's conscience in his eye—
It's my home, that's why I have these wings.

I caught their eyes.
Caught a cold glimpse of Katie at night.

If she were my sister I'd knife them.

Inside this pathetic den there's a glimpse
of Katie in a raw purple nightie.

Foamed Abandoned Conversation

Men swam naked in Barna today,
it shocked my mum.

I rewound American Psycho
to chuckle at the axe cracking you.

An indistinct week,
days of anarchic derision.

Our bodies start and stop.
We're tethered to a dimming spark.

And to so many thoughts of fear and withdrawal.

Yellow Tulips

Yellow
tulips from
Holland
yellow tulips ease
The Golden Tulip guilt
fondling memories
of red-light ladies.
The crazed young pro
endless energetic egos
speaking from crusts
boat trips to Rotterdam
sushi swivelling in pink
fleshy orifice
too
cruel
yellow
tulips
to
cheer
me
up.
I
am
far
too
sore
from
the
sun
to
look
good
for
your
return

Máire

She wasn't old.
She was old fashioned.
He wasn't fashioned.

They shopped in Dunnes
on dole day,
he obaired for the council
six months of a year,
saving the wet days,
they could shove their rain money,
he got a Gaeltacht grant.
Double-glazed windows,
schoolbooks, school uniforms,
large white St. Bernard blouses
to blanket her.
It covered survival stuff;
sarcasm, Harp lager,
Major fags and John Wayne films.
White terry towel socks
under grey mute slip-ons
with rubber uppers.

She always smiled
through thick black
rimmed Shantalla glasses,
she could read his eyes.
Harness straps shone from under her
blouse, corseting her breasts,
maiming her character further down
the Furbo shore and finally away into the sea.

Left his parked car on the prom.

She used to have fun,
she used to lick the faces of boys at Seapoint,
she used to begborrowsteal
a lift home under the stars on the Prom.

Men with dreams.
Men who knew nothing about the grant.
She's old,
she's fashioned.

She's a heavy old heap of
Ophelia bubbles in the salty sharp water.

Covering Up

Lithe tight muscles,
aching groin,
tantalite dapples
on a day for feasting.
Come over,
shackle her,
hobbled flesh teasing and
tantalizing frigid froths,
screams, whines, all-merciful whispers;
those divine silence breakers.

Feed the Dog

Feed the dog,
can you manage that?

You know where it is,
the dog food,
I've left your heart in the rabbit mix.
I think there's one in it already.
It's not mine, mine is in my rib cage,
pumping solid sweet plasma
to all my fine organs,
and my blemish-free skin,
an epidermis tough as
the heart in the rabbit heart tin.

Feed the dog,
can you manage that?

I could write it down before I parachute
from this burning bungalow.
Walk her, there's a spare tartan leash,
like the tomatoes you flushed down the drain,
green like the shirt you stained,
clogged like the mind you strayed into.

Feed the dog,
can you manage that?

It'll take you far from all that drunken
pain and whimpering moans.
And that Mensa crowd,
they don't serve you well,
all that talk of menstruation.

Feed the dog,
you can manage it.

I've left an ounce of confidence—
throw it in a yogurt,
and those screeches from the dog food can—
you can find your heart there.

Hansel and Gretel

The house tasted pleasant.
Gretel chewed gingerbread pillars,
ate until the roof rocked.
Hansel swallowed shortcake,
Gretel tendered a bone.
The witch perceived lean pickings,
Hansel conceded an arm,
soft and supple.

Gretel shoved her in an oven.
She munched another ginger heart.
Hansel took no part.

We ate so much Hansel
that we stuffed our weary world
with sweet overdoses

Rotted in cages.
Plotted bread trails.
Devoured by vultures.

Magpies

Ireland

Today I met with a dead badger,
he had a silky snout,
like a convexed chest groove.

The moment abandoned me with
an insatiable appetite to stroke it.

Slumped on ditch edge furze,
head rolled back on meaty torso,
the fed up cobra rustled.

Great prosaic vehicles went
thump thump thump
on its fleshy remains.

Iraq

Tariq drove to work today,
magpies cower overhead,
circle a child's guts and fly away.

Though the child is gold,
there is no comfort in her pale lips
or bloodstained clothes,

her body does not disappear
through melting atomic spaces
on this dirt track

as American army vans go
thump thump thump on
her fleshy remains.

Ireland

I drove to work,
magpies cowered overhead,
circling the badger's guts, gnaw his nostrils.

Swallowing whole his fluid filled eyes
in one proud muscular movement.
Birds ferociously slurping his snout
from eye socket to nostril orifice.

Though the badger is not gold,
there is a comfort in meaty prowess.
His snout proud and storable,
sensing warmth in deepening pile.

A feeling of home as he's ripped apart,
shreds on the road,
this December morning.

I Love to Read Aloud

After Thomas and Adcock

'And once below a time'

I felt that too many
binary opposites held my mind

choking in the reed high knots of theories.
They were served from a

sickening catapult of the unexplainable,
like blue berries, good for colonic health,
but why?

If we were blind and poor,
Poetics and Republic would
accompany

beans on toast, and the day to day
shit served out on
gold paper plated platters

would be consumed as if all along we
were created without bowels,
in this world of perfection.

But accept carnage, rape, and war.

Blue berry cleansings and
coffee enemas.

'But fuck it for a cheap opener'

Ice Strings

Padded twelve-year-old fat finger
pads clumped around fretting.

July, Poulnabrona.
Unbalanced like the capstone on my dolmen.
Do you remember the day I painted it?
Haunting silence with coalfish eyes?
A canvas that could cover both our bodies twice over,
but I was painting in the chapel.

Eyes behind Oakleys, shielding lust
the day we shred Lithuanian apple pie
on the top of Dun Aengus,
and I told you if you fell over
I'd fucking die laughing.

But now we've no translator.

It's easier to get an audience with Bono
and I hate those Dalkey curves.
So I'm crying in this winter palace,

strumming these ice strings
as our hell freezes.

Limerick City

In this androgynous trail of
stalking shadows,
Damo took a bus to
South Hill
driven by a pulley
for a score.
Tyres of everything in this
city are transplanted to the bellies
of mothers.
They wear vests under their skin,
teeth under their gums,
their babies under the stars
of this androgynous trail
of stalking shadows.

Limerick County

Laura only studied Domestic Science
because she liked cats.
She taught Domestic Science because
she liked teaching.
She liked drinking Fennel tea
in the Café on the first floor of Brown Thomas,
O' Connell Street, Limerick,
(In the city shop for the county girls)
where the sharp knives are kept
behind double glazed glass.
The nuns in Mary Immaculata had
a ceremony of light to celebrate
switching on Laura's halo.
She was a Domestic Science saint
after all, even with that saucy bold
red Munster jersey loose on her shoulders.
They'll get her in a habit yet.

SCBU

For Finn

You wear a prickly rash all over your furry back.
I'm not even allowed discover what you smell like,
because I have not yet become your mother.

Doctors and cleaners and candlestick makers flitter in and out.
A priest stands next to the girl with the tumor.
She's no bigger that a baby chicken.
He throws water.
Banishing these blind tiny birds from sin!

He asks me would I like a baptism,
he's a fine big boy to look so sick.
I run out screaming.

A bird next to you squeaks in a transparent incubator.

It is to be her only home.

This is the shortest ward,
here you do not walk,
there are no beds.

I'm put out again,
it's better not to see the tubes
and drips and sharp things at feeding time.
So I chat to the weeping clown on the
olive wall of the parenting room.
The TV doesn't work.
The coffee machine has been fucked against the wall.

You are naked.
The little bird speaks from inside a fabric elastoplast mask,
she stabs a twenty-four week matchstick leg to the air.

You pant to the rhythm
of an old Austrian waltz,
Ray drums, one, two, three
one, two, three,
on the rim of his paper mug.
My black roots drip over,
even now I think of my appearance.

In the lactation room my new breast friend sobs,
only a teaspoon.
Nurses reassure us it'll come sometime.
And all my thoughts of sex and
beauty and love and your eyes and looks
and flashes of stubble
and hand holding and Led Z and
The Beatles
and every missed acid trip

Of being
Of eating
Of laughing

Are distant and stained

My back is aching and my breasts
hum to the lonely bird.

MotherHeatLightMilk

but I must feed my own boy
down through a nose tube.
Little bottles in the fridge,
lined to attention like white petrol bombs
to try keep them all fired up.

MotherHeatLightMilk
This is what the world is really like—

I lie!
Welcome!
I lie!
Welcome to the world!

Letter to my Lover

Lodz,
Poland,
Winter 1997.

Moja Miłośc,

I stuck your seeping photo on the Smeg.
It held.

I haven't met a single Jew.
Daily in this universe of rational, I shiver.
The passé composé was simple
when you used to massage my temple.
Now it's all a mess.

Yesterday a flute player pulled a melody on me,
out of an iron cross that I failed to see.
A whore straddled my leg as I waited
in line for your call.

I'm trying,
trust me, I'm trying.

xxx

Diaphoresis and an Irish Girl's
New York Proposal

November, 1998

2

You
ran sweating
from the zillionth
floor of Tower One, every
thing was in zillions, it was New
York after all. But you were defunct here.
I cramped on a painful patella, the rousing ground
rocked and cried, marry me, me, me, trying to settle
your fear of heights commitment US us A and finally me.
Late autumn, holding hands two lovers jumped. A world ran

sweating
from the
zillionth
floor of T
ower One.

1

You ran sweating from the zillionth floor of Tower One,
Everything was in zillions, it was New York after all.
Large photographers snapped strange faces
in Kitsch portraits. We had packed back
so it was lame when I spoke of
Tiffany & Co., trying to settle
your fear of
heights
comm
ittme
nt
U
S
A

And
Finally
me.

Bath

I bathe in the old brown enamel bath.
It's like those olive suites from the seventies.
Only brown,
and built like a Soviet T-34.

It's chalky coarse from
Imperial Leather and Epsom salts.

Freshly cut toenails float around the
cracks from teeth and bone.
From toddler swims with my brothers,

to being alone,

discovering magazines with talk
of sex and fears.

And bullies
and lip-balm
and bath-bombs
and Clinic-shampoo

soaking for hours to
peel off oil and paint and petrol.
Steaming out tender thorns.

Heating wayward hurley bruises
hidden fag burns,
stitches from bicycle battles.

Tonight I bathe my youngest son
to relieve colic.

It will be the last swim.

Chinese Burns

Your hands grip my hoary wrists,
skin like an unused battery hen.
I'm not sure if hens have wrists
but I am certain of the counterpressure on mine,
this September evening in Lipica.

The Photograph

Goran, you poor bastard,
you stepped right into the whore's den.
You should have stuck
your peeping-Tom's-Lens
into her keyhole.

"You avert fooking
eye colleege boy.
I decen wooman
I no Slovenian hoor.
You hear me?
Avert you fooking eye".

It takes a Village to Raise a Child

The boy born with a cleft palate,
and left with a lingering lisp
to mrs and the rest Hollible Street
loved to fly kites.

Late Friday he smashed into a wall,
like a Minotaur
red nostrils
whitened eyes
flaying.

A very wrong right off.

It takes a village to raise a child.
Villages like theatres in the round
giving full-bodied audiences
bitter slurping gulps.

Audiences like chanting ranting tribes.

Villagers as preachers
unleashing Oedipal
feardapal complexes,
like spores.

Villagers as audience
members who concern
but freeze like suspended animation
on the doorstep of
twenty-two Hollible Street
because paw's on the sauce.
Not such a splendid time to sign a form.

Villagers with
creamy pockets,
selling wares
then shoving them
from windowsills.

Villagers who chomp red ribbon
with garish gold teeth,
applaud recreational areas
where rape seed plants
ravage merry-go-rounds.

It takes a village to raise a child,
shower him with chunky waxy crayons,
replaced by insecurities,
anger at graffiti.

It takes a village to suppress a soul.

The theatre lights come up,
unyielding brightness fills
nostril orifices with the reek
of burning flesh.
The audience hiss and spit,
firing rotten torrid tomatoes
on stage like clotted blood
that poured from his hands.

The hollow exposed villagers
whisper as they mop the splurge.

They wonder as they draw water to
masses in megabyte buckets.

They nail broadband to hut ceilings,
dig sewer pipes to feed one hundred channels.

They bark and neigh.

It takes a village to raise a child.

He hums through his lisp,
dragging his kite crumbling
clod over stonewalls

and hangs himself.
Two battered down Docs sway
like small black lambs in the abattoir on Good Friday.

A weight for the villagers,
a plot twist for the theatre in the round,
a plotted twist too often played.

Tea with Michael Collins

For Sinéad Murray

Sinéad, I think I was terrible wrong a stór,
I have this horrible feeling in the pit of my gut,
and I'm looking out at this rain.
Now tis indeed a mighty fine pleasure to be having
tea with you,
and you looking so well,
tis indeed a fair fine velvet hat you've on,
sure I thought you were a movie star.

I am me father's daughter, Michael

But this horrid feeling, 'twon't lift.
I just know it's all over.

Hold my hand.

They didn't get me,
my humour
and all, d'you know?
And this fecking Hiberno-
English
they're all fecking allergic to
and pretending not to understand
ah
shir tis hard get me.
I started buying our freedom with a joke.
Can you imagine it?
I didn't know how else to start it.
And of course the feckers let me start it,
a negotiating ploy,
from Oxford I'm sure,
and I've finished it,
I've finished us all.

I was all legs and arms,
like the big kettle plonked
in the midst of the china,
my suit hung like a wet sack on a spindle
and we drank the tea
with a hole for a silk thread not an Irish thumb.
Can you imagine it now;
Collins Negotiates Treaty and Tea-Cup with
Equal Measure
I made jokes
about the brass polisher and the moving
statues that served us,
and I was being honest,
and I was half fucking repentent to the hoors!

Ye fools, Ye fools, Ye have left us
our Fenian Dead!

Why didn't I sing them that?
Why the guilt?
Drink up your tea now.
How was the train ride?

Tis a bad feeling I have altogether,
oh Sinéad,
a bad feeling in my pit of my gut,
that I finished it all off.
I'm terrible sorry a stór.
Terrible sorry…'

Shaking Hands

He told me in December as a fairy light
about to crack
that I wasn't to kiss him in the schoolyard anymore.
He requested as an awkward lover
that we shake hands on parting.

Red Stiletto

For Andrea

Hustles of whistling whispering girls,
hair straight as sheets of tarred glass
and breasts taut and shy to the Autumn breeze.

She carried her jacket,
arms above her head like an African woman
with her last pail of evening water.

We greet as everyday, with honesty.

Unsettling nerves fill the small space,
knees jerking,
polka dots jumping from her socks.

Half a bottle of vodka
and your red stillettos are required
for Junior Cert results celebration.
Please.

The Little Boys on the News

The little boys on the Six One news are naked,
everyone knows they are naked,
boxes hide their nakedness
boxing out their bodies in
large Rice Krispie squares.

The little boy on the news is just
like the little boy beside me,
except he has lost his mother
and another has taken to minding him,
matting his hair
and dressing him in camouflage.

There are millions of boxed Rice Krispie bit like boys,

And nobody hears
And nobody sees
And nobody tastes
And nobody touches
And nobody smells

but everything in this world slowly rots.

The Polish have Caused a Crash

The Polish have caused a crash
on the boreen
between Whites
and the old house.
And Brazilians
have opened a new
Mexican restaurant beside
Molloys.
Even the Chinese chef
is giving out.
There isn't a car with tax
and not one of the new ones
are putting a thing into her economy
shopping in Aldi.
They'll screw up the new children
with their gutter genes.
John Nolan even told me
the same thing happened when
the farmers mixed Freisians
and Belgian Blues.
The unreal moo's outta the fuckers
and everyone knew it was
because they weren't true blue.
The new priest has
lady callers
with tracksuits
and bling,
pink nails
and blow up beds.
He thinks nothing
of drinking the new coffee in
Mocha Beans.
tis fucked entirely we are
entirely fucked.

Carats

Nails bitten below bloody quick,
soft pink wet fleshy flesh.
I gnaw
a sleepy wedding finger.

A gauche mount of Venus
on my plump hand,
interrupted by a lone freckle.

I'm carat-less and
awkward to the grocery rain and hail.
Feeding spores and my
incomplete Sundays.

Flirt

In Nairobi,
a beautiful black man
is asking the village cattle farmer
for his daughter's hand in marriage.

He needs a third wife—
to tend his growing herd.

(Lucky Bastard)

In front of me
at chipboard desks—
leaning against walls with no plaster—
I ask the class to discuss
representation of women in Lear—

unrealistic.

(Can we
separate
the playwright
from the play?)

I close my lids
like cranky shutters on
a busy telly-shop front to imagine him.

I try hard to recreate his face.
Beginning with his eyes—
in strokes I make my way to
his mouth
and then it all disappears.

I start over again, and over again.

At the back of the class
a mosher punches a traveller.

In my report I tell the truth—
I saw nothing.
I had my eyes closed.

Gaza

After William Carlos Williams

A little girl tips her wheelbarrow of
rubble on the base of the water pump.

A big boy raises his arm through a hole
in a turquoise wife-beater top,
and launches it
like a foam rocket,
high above his head.

His underarm hair is wet and knotted
and it's the last thing the girl sees
until hot blood runs from her temple.

Open gasp
Little girl
Tastes

Relief

For all the while the blood had made them scream
around her and made her afraid.

Relief

Her first taste

Relief

Small dark ankles like frog eyes
stand straight in yellow short socks.
She brushes down her dress,
walks towards the dusty street
like a snapshot with a red veil.

water precious
water precious
water precious
water precious

The boy screams at an NGO,
kicks his bucket to heaven
screaming his screams.

Like willow branches her ankles wave
and bend in their yellow roots.

Snap.

The little girl drops like

the plastic bullets all around her,
slumps on her wheelbarrow,
upon which so much depended.

Blood

For survivors of church abuse

I am a seven year old man
on a green wet seat in
Cricklewood.

I am drinking tea from Subway,
my stubble is itchy.
I am thinking of my mother.
I see her face in every young woman
that passes me,
scolding children
wiping their noses
grabbing their hands
from the ends of
little thin arms out through gillet holes,
long wispy hair.

I am climbing the tree in the park,
I balance the tea paper cup between my teeth
and from up high I know I'll get a better view.
Maybe I will find her.
And we can play bow and arrows
and she can run up
the street in her heels
and red coat
and be the Indian
chased by her cowboy
and I will aim at her
but it won't hurt.

I am seven years old and I have the hairy sheet
over my head so
they'll think I'm dead.

I saw a dead man once in
the corpse house.
I was polishing the brass
and they wheeled him in,
just like that.
I don't know did he look more like one of them
or a ghost.

I am seven years old
walking through the aisles of
Iceland,
counting my change with my hand in my pocket.
I have enough to
buy a frozen steak and kidney
pie
and a small carton of milk.
I buy some cider in the
off licence on the corner.
I ask the woman behind the counter
is there any chance she may be my mother.
She doesn't speak,
maybe she's deaf.

My mother was tall,
with a red coat and a
blue hat.
We took the bus to Galway
and then another to Letterfrack.
I could make things there,
she said
It was a much better school
than the one in Dublin,
she said
and she said that the birds stay
up all night in Letterfrack
calling to her brothers and sisters
in Boston—

It's only over the sea,
she said
and when they call back
that'll be them talking to me,
she shows me pictures from her tan purse
and tells me their names—
she's told me before
but I never remember, sure
I'm only seven,
I haven't even lost my top teeth yet.

I tell her that I'm lonely,
and what if there's blood when I lose
my top teeth?

She grabs my hand and
tells me the teachers will wrap them
in blue tissue paper—
she's it packed in my bag
and to put them under the pillow.

I never see the blue tissue paper
I never see my mother
I never hear the Letterfrack birds at night time

and if I do they're screaming like dying crows
being killed to scare themselves
being beat under a flour sack
in the backyard of a farmer's house.

I never see blood from my top teeth,
I only see the blood
that runs down the
backs of my legs
and the only blue I see
is the toilet walls
while I rub away the blood.

I am seven,
I am climbing a tree in Cricklewood
I am rubbing the blood from my small thigh.

I will build a tree-house up
here
I will hammer these branches together
and nail each one
to another.
I can stay up here
with the closed-in branches
and the view.
It can be a sort of a tree house.
I hold the cup steady between my teeth
as I hammer,
trying not to spill a drop.
I'll have it for supper
and then I can go
to bed
and cover my head.
I can feel the rain drip dropping—
but it's water
and I am safe
here in my house.
Not one will hear me
and not one will come
and the branches will hold me tight,
me and my tea
and I know that I will see
my mother up here.

Mea culpa
Mea culpa
Mea culpa

I know I will see my mother from up here.

Basement Rave

Klub Hotel, Lipica, Slovenia

The critics here
the two of them—
don't criticise
preferring steak kebabs
on steely skewers
and Pellegrino for breakfast with
bubbles for after
and pineapple rings
with the odd comment on post—
modernism
and structured Slovenian
wine drank
by the neck with
tarry like tannins—
shouting about Eastern European
film and their own
sexuality—
honest discourse of
every boy they came in
shouting out through
slobbery wet lips.

His Mother prefers boys
when the boys stay over—

Father prefers girls
if the girls bend over—

he'll take any bit
of anything else
after a few bottles
of Chianti
on a Saturday evening—

when he becomes a
night angel in Flemish—
on a flight from
memories of first times.

The two Chinese
sit on a stone
swopping phermones
out the back—
sure why not
where they discuss
foot binding
strewn beautifully together
through the ends of their hair
making one head—
and the prison cell
memory comes up again—
so for him
I dance Riverdance
to promote the country
I would read but
they can't hear me
and it's dancing they want
they've had enough
fucking poetry—
to chants of
come on EERish
dance fa me EERish girl
I love kivinagh
almost as much as myself

I dance like a battering ram on Firefly
in this mahogany basement
when even my eyes have gone out—
where the commie-rats have been replaced
by musty old hippy boys
gyrating at my leg—
Ginsberg's on the TV

that curves like a pregnant egg—
he's bracing himself to come join me
and take the glassy bottle
off the tranny
spinning it round on the floor
and shout
WAKE UP FOOLS
WAKE UP—
RIGHT NOW FOLKS
PLEEEAASSSE

My dead Granny shoves
a lemon to my hand
to cut the taste of raw liquor—
she drank five gins to a tonic
it's not licked from the wind
and we lick from the sky here
together.

My arse cheeks are
clapping a beat
to the vibrate of
Talking Heads—
I can speak French

I can't seem to face up to the facts.
I'm tense and nervous and I… can't relax.
I can't sleep, cause my bed's on fire.
Don't touch me I'm a real live wire.

Psycho Killer
Qu'est-ce que c'est?
fa fa fa fa fa fa fa fa fa fa better
Run run run run run run run away
OH OH OH

Smoke fags backwards
gyrate like Madonna

fly to the sky of
the roof top terrace—
where they keep the dead horses
and cheese mould

and the books on
Bukowski and
Friel

we're rounding our lips
in a tribal dance for
a Christian—
Pagan convert priest
puckering together
like three legged
Lippazaners—
throwing clonking
loose limbs to the air—
to the table
as a meat served
up in a halter of freedom—
licking sweat and love and
secret parts
holding skinny slips
of European things with steel plates
for bellies.

Oh the souls have come to party me
hear my secrets

let me tell you a secret
let me tell you a secret

the angels are bollocks
only things for a crisis
just as a
worry stone or
herbal pill

in this base basement—
dead hotel
you'd hear secrets
if you could hear
and see devils if you
could see.

We will leave without sleep
in three wheelers
by chauffeurs
talking socialism
re-bordering
and horses in the meadows
a dead ghost of a
passing of promise and product
stolen only
by another country
with balls to capture it
all—

shaky and silly
sore and afraid—
in places not named
to whispering madness
if you insist on throwing
and thrusting yourself
around on top of me
you'll be sore!
Too true
but did you enjoy it?

Bleeding from all the
cells of the cremated
through the eyes
and the brain
to a stain
that leaves a phase
in a haze of no doubt
but uncertainty.

Will we re-mime Riverdance
talk as culchies on Poppers
re-align the Chinese pair
pick them up
and peel them off
the wet clouds they've morphed into
feet intact—
Marlboro red dead ends
in a little red book in the ash tray
with grass sweet ends
that would burn the tongue of a novice.

———————————————

Alive, barely
in Trieste
at noon
off a powered white bus
to a Sunday of screaming
nothingness—
gathering our lives in a bag
ashamed and afraid—
like the red nameless
flowers on some man's
temporary grave.
The streets here crawl
with the invisible
the fan in the room
only whirring life
save the minibar.

I look for the mafia
but settle for a pizza

sit with a lager in a city of
invisible
sit with Joyce on the street

near the market
sit on a path outside a
church up a backstreet
sit for a vomit on a pavement
near a tavern
sit with the shakes
and a feeling of strangeness

share my lager with the street vendor Marco
share my mind with the spirit of Samuel
share my skin with the Gods of forgotten
share my party with the paranoid monkeys
share Slovenia with a younger Svetlana
share euros with tangled old gypsies
share my lipstick with only the street air
where I'm beautifully gorgeous
an evening
mess
on the cure

Song lyrics in Italics from Talking Heads

Time

For five days, eight months, two weeks
some hours,
I have thought of little else.

I have a wobbly stomach,
it hobbles like a piece of carpet fluff in the Spring sun.
I have a sweaty face.
And although I believe my brain is firmly inside my skull
for five weeks, eight hours and some days
I've worked hard at convincing myself.

My mouth is dry, and I flip my words.
I'm as an awkward box of air.
I can neither stand up
or fall over.
I can neither see
or be felt.

For some time now I have been leaving.
I am coming away from this place.

I feel my own tears.
I clamp my eyes shut.

For some time now
I have felt every moment
my body moved.
Each heavy footfall,
or eyelash jitter.
These motions as a part of me
and you
and if my piece of everything I planned
should shudder
or crash
in a kind of a shuddery crash,

then everything with matter
and everything that matters

will crumble down,
as a biscuit

a well of doom
our castle wall under siege.

The redness that builds on my skin
with immeasurable pain over my breasts
to try to keep me calm,
to try to rouse me from this state
and investigate
and say
hey, it's okay
we all feel this way
sometimes

But for five hours, eight months, two years
and ten minutes

I have thought of little else.

My red eyes look back
at their own reflection.
And I know that
when I reach out and touch me
it is only then
that I will truly die.

About the Author

ELAINE FEENEY was born in Galway in 1979. She studied English and History at University College Galway and completed post graduate study in University College Cork and University of Limerick. She has been writing since her early teens. In 2006 she won the North Beach Nights Grand Slam and in 2008 won the Cuirt Festival's Poetry Grand Slam. She is a keen page and  performance writer. Elaine has performed at many venues including The Edinburgh Fringe Festival, The Electric Picnic, The Vilenica Festival and The Cúirt International Literature Festival. She was the chosen writer on a One Sheet collaboration in 2010 with an artist and a graphic designer and this work is currently on exhibit across Dublin. Her work has been translated into Slovene. Elaine lives in Athenry with her partner Ray, and sons, Jack and Finn.